Dealer's Choice

Selected Poems 1993-2012

by
James Aaron Tecumseh Sinclair

**PUBLISHED IN
GALLOWAY, OHIO USA**

Dealer's Choice
Selected Poems 1993-2012

All rights reserved.

This work, or portions thereof,
may not be reproduced in any form
without the written permission of the author.

All poems in this volume were originally published in
Artifacts- A Book Poetical (2010),
Simple Little Things: 365 Volumes 1-12 (2012), or
Dealer's Choice (2015)
by Masked Man Media.

Copyright 2015
By
James Aaron Tecumseh Sinclair

Second Edition

Published 2015

ISBN 978-1517174637

Table of Contents

When I Die 1
Lost to Chemistry 3
Awkward Prompts 4
Dragonfly 5
Morning Hymn 6
Left Drifting 7
Suburban Ale 8
Upon the Trail 9
Sunday 10
Wag Dog Park 11
Ritual 12
Route 42 13
Halloween 14
Where Dinosaurs Grazed 15
Little Man 16
Back Again 17
Oracle 18
Meningitis 19
Riverside 20
Translator 21
Hear Me Through 22
Cayman 23
Aisle Toddler 24
Padded Bras 25
Cravings 26
Insomnia 27
Seven 28
Micro 29
Necromancy 30
Denny's 31
Urban Decay 33
Nightwatch 35
Pigeon 36
Indulgence 37

Undeterred *39*
Evolution *41*
Static *42*
Friendly Intervention *43*
Haunted *45*
Last Poem *51*
Third Person Myths *52*
Genesis *53*
Modern Love *55*
Daven *56*
Baruch Ata Adonai *57*
Feet Apart *58*
Birth *59*
Little Sweets *60*
One Day *61*
The Hanging Tree *62*
These Pages *63*
Duck *64*
Missing *65*
Snow, Moon, Jupiter, Anne *66*
Daedalus *67*
Parking *68*
Metrophobic Sabrage *69*
Missed Connections *71*
Momma *72*
Old Plains *73*
Southern Cross *74*
Wine *78*
Premise *79*
Porn Shop *80*
Moment *81*
Chemistry *82*
Lot's Wife *83*
Modest Orb Weaver *84*

When I Die

Originally titled- December 6, 2011

when I die, adorn my body
with props and gags
hire a stage manager to send queues
behind the casket to the fly-master
who'll raise my left arm up and down
as gawkers pass, lift my arm
for a goodbye wave or high five,
organize lottery drawings out
of the crowds favorite orifice,
staple electrodes to the corners of my lips,
wire me to the internet, let me smile
for strangers with push button convenience,
wallpaper the wake with my ponderous poetry,
unfortunate sober ramblings coughed forth by
ego, place hidden tweeters in corners
whispering stumbling Shakespearian
monologues just audible for those seeking
randy ghosts, ready the helium filled airbags
under my prayer shawl, allow them to inflate,
carry me above the mourners, bouncing bloated
metronome rolling along the ceiling toward
open skylights, hatched to sunshine, a new bird
taking flight dodging 747s and contrails,
shrunken genitals kissing clouds as I
reach the barest edges

of space

lungs expanding

skin shiny with ice

ears deaf to the thin winds

stellar life preserver pop-
ping from the expanse

my stiff fleshy remains thawing, crunching

as I land neck first in a field
found by vagrant housecats succumbing
to temptations of human flesh, tiny toothy
revenges for years of hard food,
found by fathers and sons encountering
adventure crumpled by a drainage ditch,
found by curious blind tea party foraging girls,
armed with bags of makeup and hope,
all in heavenly chorus
reciting the note that says,
"If found, call-"
activating the cell phone in my mouth
baritone otherworld ringing,
leave a message at the beep,
beep,
share the number so my mouth keeps singing
allow me to become your savior from spam-
bots, auto-dialers and scammers, humming
under hundreds of layers of paint
massaged over me by sororities
until I become a bug trapped in amber

Lost to Chemistry

Originally titled- March 6, 2012

over cards and wine glasses
saucy old women pull sagging skin into smiles
remember giggles and sneaking smokes
check out waiters younger than grandkids

saucy old women pull sagging skin into smiles
that had seemed too thick for their faces
check out waiters younger than grandkids
forgetting widowed vows, old lovers smiles

that had seemed too thick for their faces
last seen in a box, lips molded like putty
forgetting widowed vows, old lovers smiles
lost to chemistry

last seen in a box, lips molded like putty
the ladies check their makeup, check their hearts
lost to chemistry
over cards and wine glasses

Awkward Prompts

Originally titled- December 29, 2011

Chintzy paint man-
ufacturer mixing pigments, poems,
marketing obscure amalgams
in color theory

Indigenous Peoples, Rustic Mystery Collections
Warm Neutrals Brown
Drink fertility through
brooks brokering simplicity
digest visions over
smoldering cooking fires, run
naked, run free
Irrigation

Winter Delight, Northern Treasures Collections
Cool Blues
Fly high as a Jet
tuning your palate on The Fork
Succulent muds canoed by Cree
under cool stars, bartering food,
furs, fables
Winnipeg

Cozy Kitchens, Eccentric Lifestyle Collections
Reds
Succulent and salty
like an old lovers kiss
carving hearts,
savor, remember,
each tasting the same as the next
Cannibalism

Dragonfly

For Cori- Valentine's Day 2009

Adam must have
felt it, the deep
visceral movement under
his chest- his heart
fluttering

dancing
like the vow-
els of his first speech,
one that was like him

prancing from the darkness,
this divine spark laying
consonants in his chords
mingling with his

song: an unpredictable
entwining of melodies

her toes could skip
her hips could sway
her lips could shape
her tongue could savor-

and he must
have sat
and swooned as I do
now, seeing you smile

Morning Hymn

Originally titled- May 12, 2012

breath of the morning
permeating clothes, nose,
oily earthy wafts
burbling boiling
jitter-bitters percolating
kissing ceramic and cream
muffling spoony clinks
steam lifting offerings
accepted through lips, through
teeth, slurps,
hums hymns
hallelujah for coffee

Left Drifting

Originally titled- January 3, 2012

you who were
born under a fat orange moon
leave me here drifting
the elongated shores of lake erie
leaning over the edge
listening for distant soft slaps
along crusty dilapidated docks
missing their many fish like i caught
one summer as a boy when
the mussels were less
parched and asking you to dance
was the great sucking fear
long ago before we met long ago
before the tangles of your hair dug into my
shoulder long ago before sweaty twisted
flailings in the dark
long ago before you and i shared
secrets resting on fossil filled
outcroppings stretching
placid high waters long ago
you i miss the most
you i miss while searching
glimmering night waters

Suburban Ale

Originally titled- November 11, 2011

Last of the amber
hoppy fall ale
soaking fabricated flesh-
toned thrift store rug inside,
as we sit desanitizing winter's
air on cement stoop ice flows lips
spewing smoke and mist and story
searching for the hunter over
industrial street lamps ill-
uminating frosted roofs in suburbia

Upon the Trail

Originally titled- June 23, 2012

our answers lie upon the trail
canopied beneath the tree line veil
sharing sunbeams where robins fly
where lovers brace and clouds drift by
and asphalt heat cures all who ail

who cry for help to no avail
whose weathered boots give toes their sail
their knotted dreams they can't untie
our answers lie upon the trail

the bones uncrack, mad hearts prevail
if sunlight falls, the moon won't fail
guide us to heaven caressing the sky
sanctuary of stars which too will die
though the touch of death we can't curtail
our answers lie upon the trail

Sunday

Originally titled- February 26, 2012

Sunday kitchen, son
wears floppy socks, twirls
over blond laminate wood, sings
after eating angel hair pasta,
while she sloshes dish water,
her back and booty
to me, her eyes thanking
the sunset

Wag Dog Park

Originally titled- March 16, 2012

Inside the husk, licked by fires,
painted with scorches and tear drops,
vagrants sleep & keep camp,
wrapped in the living

tree, sucking sweet stream water
detoured from the Darby, filtered
up & through
gnarled branches

outstretching holey canopy,
like their hands, a hallelujah to the sun
another day living another day
awoken by the chattering
symphony of birds

Ritual

Originally titled- January 15, 2012

Spicy incense sticks jabbed
soft soil at the cardinal points,
musky oils succumbing to slight
fires rolling down lithe metal shafts,
releasing thin curls chasing solstice
breezes, these prayers

surrounding, drifting over grasses
toward a bored moon, smoky snakes
breaking into webbed fingers
wishing for cloud cover, light-

ning weighty rains to cleanse this iron
bridge or transform it in-
to rust, end its vigil as I

squat along its stone found-
ation envision his
possibilities within
this sweaty cauldron of smoke,
Joshua, first
offspring sacrificed, I enjoin
it's fetal spirit to forgive
and forgive, and forgive, and for
her, primal archetype, for her
whose womb succumbed
to mercenaries, mind
contrition exercised through
progenies, especially those testing

embryonic tongues.

Dealer's Choice

Route 42

Originally titled- October 15, 2011

You are Route 42 drifting
before me in a haze of smoldering
acrid tobacco, effortless,
as I pray between the steady thump-
kerthump-thump of purring 2 am tires
in the deep back-
woods dark, tears baptizing me.
Coasting
into a super-
market, this harbor
of light, evangelical
as I carry the feel of you
around me, an apostle mooring
beneath massive lights, casting
alms of smoke to blizzards of moths

Halloween

Originally titled- October 31, 2011

sweaty late fall streets,
besieged by fairies, we skipped
between islands of porch light
along cement bones

begging for sweets.
skirting barren
trees, their leaves slick,
moldy afghans
insolating their roots,
my son chose
a dark between place

to silence our ramblings,
speak in serious tones.
had I ever stood for something
unpopular, had to defend it.
we know intuitively
that is the test that delineates
Boy from Man, and all I could
recall were tiny treasons of cowardice.

Where Dinosaurs Grazed

Originally titled- September 9, 2012

his cup
not full, alone in
the almost dark of nightlight
surrounded by black
shiny eyes buried
in stuffed faces- lions,
wolves, strong
animals peering over his collapsing
shoulders (his back a shell, like the turtle,
protective and calloused
thanks to the evolutions of pain)
toddler within the pre-teen seeking
old words carved into yellowed pulp, sung
by his curly haired mother
when times were less
divided, when the flowers she planted
grew in a place he called home
where rocks held magic
where trees spoke in squirrel tongue
where dinosaurs grazed with buicks

Little Man

Originally titled- March 13, 2012

Monkey, dyed
purple from swims in
pigment contaminated pools
by moonlight, finds
new shapes
swimming the Pollack-splattered
firmament as his
feet sink in organic pond muck

reminiscent, he calls, as ancestors
form in the skies,
his
        lungs
                spasm,
a young musician un-
certain of his wood-
wind, his
voice lifts, a
first thought beyond immediacy
into inevitability
little man
connecting

Back Again

Originally titled- June 5, 2012

succulent strappy heels,
prance-enabling prosthetics,
shellacked
with the innards of cherries
whose stems ingested glitter,
click-clacking cement,
crunching pebbles, foraging
for the thirties,
for deco,
for marble,
bypassing gum & oily puddles,
sniffing for leather
soles
toes rise to sky
& back again, dashing
suits, practitioners of dance
& old world
chivalry, skipping
5th Street, past
wails of hopscotch & whiffs of bread,
three more blocks to an empty nest

Oracle

Originally titled- May 27, 2012

Little slow chipmunk,
midsection smashed by tires
dispersing weighty
cyclist chatting on cell phone,
you lived more than most of us,

surrounded by trees
savoring sweet grass and nuts
chatting with blue jays
before your innards became
natures, recycled fly food,

laying wide eyed, blind,
furry curiosity
mouth stuck in a scream
small prophet announcing our
inevitability

Meningitis

Originally titled- December 24, 2011

You are my bacterial meningitis, coming
quickly, leaving
fever and chills, severe
headache, bulging
fontanelles, decreased consciousness,
mental status change, unusual
posture punctuated
by nausea, requiring
hospitalization

Riverside

Originally titled- March 1, 2012

you lift the iridescent shell from the soft almost
sandy riverbed, alone without the other half,
your breathing and the shushing rapids drape
over pale grasses hugging awkward trees
contemplating their last polar bear dive, waters
clear, inviting as pain to numb fingers, fish
burrowed beneath algae muds adorned in
broken green glass, sensing heat, coming
elongated days, electric chemistry of mating
           flooding reveals old
           hand wrought rusted iron chains
           age withers confinements

Translator

Originally titled- June 13, 2012

what, no corporate
poets, no tinkers,
striking clarity
from business-speak stone
no market for such
things, not when you have

synergy and par-
adigm shifts leverag-
ing win-win deliv-
erables, not when
bases can be touched
by resourceful team
players, procuring
human resources.

who then, devises
thirty second pitch
sessions, tag lines, im-
mortal catchphrases,
repeated mantras,
even when the pro-
duct is resigned, songs,
jingles, catchy hymns
fossils as to what
our hearts used to be

Hear Me Through

Originally titled- August 26, 2012

In secret I speak
To you, think you hear me through
The trees, orange leaves
Tumbling over rotted
Nuts, sticky pine cones,
Brown needles sanitizing
Rings 'round conifers
That drink light through steely shafts
Just enough to see
And as the wind starts to bend
And creak knurled trunks
I pretend you whisper back
As for an instant
I'm the sharp universal
Focal point lucky
Enough to deserve cosmic
Homily, but then
The predator finds its prey
And nest loses egg
And bikes pass and people talk
The woods grow quiet
And I alone walk away
Back the way I came
Over litter and white bones
Both still, forgotten
Embarrassed I thought I earned
Single attention
Unique confirmation I
Could share passing those
Alone in the deep dark wood

Cayman

Originally titled- January 29, 2012

puffy cat face more
wide than tall, orange maine coon
snorts his displeasure
no fan of my poetry
regardless of its stroking

Aisle Toddler

Originally titled- January 13, 2012

grubby little thing
babbling curses
jabbing its chubby
oily fingers at paparazzi-puke-slathered
commerce, its flabby
breasted progenitor perusing cheap
tobaccos, sugar waters,
jonesing for a cultural high,
bobble-headed evolutionary cuteness
preventing paternal infanticide, generously
sized ocular orbs wet,
asking over slick lips,
pardon, asking for merci-
ful kidnapping

Padded Bras

Originally titled- December 13, 2011

Seven year olds in padded bras
bringing sexy back,
eyes ringed in masc-
ara, tiny thonged hips gyrating
before their bodies can conceive
womanhood, defined by adornment
and utility, little
princess daughters
sitting on porches, swinging
their thin legs, singing hymns
to hotness waiting for ruling
princes.

Cravings

Originally titled- November 22, 2011

She lays by me, her womb
craving fatty sweets
sucking to the metal-
lic conclusion of iced cream,
chocolate, raspberry
spoonfuls heated and melted
by her greedy fat tongue, her chest
goose pimpled as she tries to restrain
herself while scooping and giggling

Insomnia

Originally titled- December 18, 2011

Morning moon near Spica
and Saturn before dawn,
whirling double star casting breezes
these pajama scrubs a cool cocoon
while reading driftwood tea leaves
floating in herbal backwash
mourning the death of sleep

Seven

Originally titled- July 24, 2012

seven, you're my seven,
front line winner seven
how you no the field
and take the don'ts
pay my line, save our odds
as working bets have action
paid behind
every time

Micro

Originally titled- November 20, 2011

within the water of my
eye micro-
organisms swim, black
and grey
in a field of pounding
white as I stare
at a street lamp through tears,
this little universe
base and blissful, held between
matted eyelashes unaware
they prism a slideshow
of you, of you, of you

Necromancy

Originally titled- March 4, 2012

Off they go
to church, her
to sing
and rejuvenate, give
praise, receive
comfort, he
to mingle and posture
as pre-teens do, full
of awkward bravado through
inexperience as I
conjure bits and bytes
into letters, craft sigils
into syllables, conduct
the necromancy of poetry

Denny's

Originally titled- February 29, 2012

Over her first
        cup of coffee,
                she lived
one bedroom
        flat, solitary
                windowsill big
enough for dust,
        two chairs. Deep red
                brick exterior, chipped
white paint trim.

Over her second
        cup of coffee,
                first bummed
smoke, her
        mother slept away
                cancer in her living
room. Old woman's
        possessions boiled
                down to a scattering
windowsill plants,
        castaways plucked from soft
                soils, gardens planted
first year she was
        married. When she did experience
                wake-
fulness, the woman remembered
        dancing sun breezes,
                stories
of a tall man carrying her
        over thresholds.

Dealer's Choice

Over her third
> cup of coffee,
>> steam and silence.

Over her fourth
> cup of coffee,
>> second bummed cigarette,

she recalled the deep
> night quiet
>> sitting alone

the body, her mother,
> waiting for someone to take
>> her away, breezes which carried

scents of soil minerals.

Over her fifth
> cup of coffee,
>> she counted

numbers and varieties
> plants still on her
>> sill, colors, characters,

reminding her of simple
> things, living
>> things, all in need,

all to tend. This, she
> explained, is why
>> she kept flowers on her

windowsill.

Urban Decay

Originally titled- November 17, 2011

pregnant night sky, fetuses
pressing rotund clouds
sloshing in watery sacks
appendages and faces casting in-
coherent sigils earthward,
parched brick and cement
agape and cracked in anticip-
atory chill, alone next to flashing yellow signals
musty alleys swept by dust devils
pygmy trees outstretched in nude celebration
frozen leaves skipping down streets with-
out right of way, holy tanned sails
summersaulting over remnants of cigarette
butts, dead grass, food wrappers
here in the heart of impoverished cityscape
here where crimes of destitution and despair
pose as the hustle and bustle of commerce
here before the sun
screws up the courage to shine
here night skies birth quenching rain,
drop signs of renewal from the heavens
soothe spongy brick
here pungent stench is blown clean
here trees rejoice in the dark, leaves confetti,
tap-dancing blacktop stages
here, now, wickedness is illusory
substantive as a postcard

evil does not lurk, because man
does not lurk

Nightwatch

Originally titled- July 14, 2012

Should I go ahead and brush my teeth
Grab teddy and climb into bed
Think you can pray over me
As I line my army
To watch through the night
I'm scared of death
Again, scared
It finds
You

Pigeon

Originally titled- July 8, 2012

pigeon, who nested at lane
avenue, under the 315 bridge,
you dodged right, left, right,
certain as your eyes and heart would allow
riding the median dashes between
swift black tires
bobbing your head, glistening green and blue,
forgetting how to fly,
in my rear view mirror, implanted
into asphalt by a truck
too large, or too cruel
to swerve

Indulgence

Originally titled- October 28, 2011

Jamboree kicked off in a violet mist
of tentacles slapping, trunks bleating kazoos,
fleshsack ornaments clanking,
clipped to miscellaneous appendages
functioning as toes, eyelids, fingernails,
tattoos.

Gods macro and nano
licked language into emissaries bounding
between atmospheres vomiting celestial
commerce. All of them Lord, Lady, Most
High, The One, The Many, Creat-
ors, The Ancients, in whatever epist-
emological construct that would contain
them, massaged and copulated, as winds
of prayer basted over their skins-shells-
gelatins from indulgent minor organisms
concerned with rudimentary superstitions
like behavior, self-purpose, castes,
plagues, righteousness.

Comparing glyphs Jamboreeans a-
ttempted to legislate equitable intra-organism
supplication bylaws, entitlements paid as
magic and miracle, further fraudulences
conspired, wrapped in onion paper like thin
stones bleeding convoluted mythologies,
distractions until consensus could be bartered
between lofty courts.

Sustenance born from the sym-
phony of the Great Beginning
fled as hurdling red shift

Dealer's Choice

inked the firmament. Their sins
accelerated their worlds like repelling
magnets, dark energies breeding mass, places
between where manna dwelt drifted to pulsar
pastures away from ignorant mucus sack
throats. They were
starving from indulgences.

All of them.

Undeterred

Originally titled- June 28, 2012

Hey black and blue, it's me again today
I've heard what you thought you had to say
You said I can't be ok
Can't keep these demons at bay
Live life my own way

But these are my words
Wrote them down to save their sound
Planted them in white pulp ground
Where they flower undeterred

I love her smile, the curls of her hair,
I love her son, his heart in prayer,
I love this life, I'm not ashamed,
I love this life, leaving it unnamed,

Hey black and blue, it's me again today
Heard you knock on my rainy day
Remind me that I'm made of clay
Got some debts I can't repay
One day I'll decay

But these are my words
Wrote them down to save their sound
Planted them in white pulp ground
Where they flower undeterred

I love her smile, her skin so fair,
I love her son, seeing myself there
I love this life, I'm not ashamed
I love this life, leaving it unnamed

But these are my words
Wrote them down to save their sound
Planted them in white pulp ground
Where they flower undeterred

With them I'm never far from home
I lose the definition of alone
Feel a warmth within my bones
My heart finds its metronome

Hey black and blue, lookin' muddy today
Heard you might be turning gray
Think your scar might go away
Weak down to your DNA
Gotta walk, I cannot stay

But these are my words
Wrote them down to save their sound
Planted them in white pulp ground
Where they flower undeterred

With them I'm never far from home
I lose the definition of alone
I love this life, I'm not ashamed
I love this life, leaving it unnamed

But these are my words
Wrote them down to save their sound
Planted them in white pulp ground
Where they flower undeterred

Dealer's Choice

Evolution

Originally titled- May 23, 2012

what time was it when
evolution established
your trajectory
what creatures receive thanks for
delivering you to me.

Static

Originally titled- May 2, 2012

Unable to dial in to the divine
frequency, sputtering divinations
revealing not so much
a burning match or testimonial ant hill
cursing the luck of Moses' fireside chat
I sit cross-legged alone in the rain
which slithers cool minty fingers over my
pale body, I
tweak a dial in my swollen mind
Its stubby toothy cylinder caked
gray, slathered in skin cells,
listening for a sullen Buddha, a fiery Jesus,
a laughing Mohammad, a squishy Zeus, any
signal to break
the loneliness between bickering brain
segments, all of them resting their reason on in-
complete tablets of understanding, huddled
together in the ivory cave praying for direct-
ion to come from without
a murmur or song
to hum above the tip-e-tap raindrops
and self-flagellation of storms

Friendly Intervention

Originally titled- April 25, 2012

A little friendly intervention
Avoid boring superstition
Embrace a cloudy day
Don't be shy to shiver & shudder
Steer the boat without a rudder
Let them go their separate way

> Be scared to death
> Take a deep breath
> Listen to confessions
> From unusual directions

A little friendly intervention
Avoid dishonest intention
Embrace each word you say
Don't be shy to bend & ache
Steer your heart toward words that break
Let them go their separate way

> Be scared to death
> Take a deep breath
> Listen to confessions
> From unusual directions

We all kiss the stars, eventually
No concept of eternity
Just something from afar
And from where we are
No certainty
Certainly
Live now
Today

> Be scared to death
> Take a deep breath
> Listen to confessions
> From unusual directions

A little friendly intervention
Avoid clever invention
Embrace those older ways
Don't be shy to dance & sing
Steer away from tentative things
Let them go their separate way

> Be scared to death
> Take a deep breath
> Listen to confessions
> From unusual directions

> Be scared to death
> Take a deep breath
> Listen to confessions
> From unusual directions

A little friendly intervention

> Be scared to death
> Take a deep breath
> Listen to confessions
> From unusual directions

A little friendly intervention
Avoid dishonest intention
Embrace each word you say
Don't be shy to bend & ache
Steer your heart toward words that break
Let them go their separate way

Let them go their separate way

Let them go their separate way

Dealer's Choice

Haunted

Originally titled- October 12, 2011

I

Some people swore
the house was haunted.

Cats had fluffed their fur
in open windows. Hushed
giggles had sliced the night
as young dreamers scattered
their wishes across a sea
of shorn grass, bodies silvered
under a harvest moon.
Where hydrangeas once puffed
their snowballs lingered
parched ivy, spider sacs, shattered
clay pots.

II

Some people swore
the house was haunted.
Neighbors sometimes

approached and
pressed their fingers in-
to the cracked doorbell.

He watched them kick aside
cigarette butts, debate

with each other as they peered up
at him through the sheers.

"Take a pear," they heard.
"Help yourself," they heard.
A lighter snapped. Ice
found a glass.

III

Some people swore
the house was haunted.
Sometimes

at night, they slipped
passed him as he s w a y e d
on his lawn, his toes
wet, his lips whispering
mantras. They pretended
to round the corner, looked over
their shoulders and around junipers,
watched as his hands
search his pajamas.
They knelt low, hushed themselves
as he produced a Ziploc
bag. He stopped, sat cross-
legged in the dew. His fingers
pinched and flung grey powder at
the base of the young pear tree.
They shepherded themselves
down a cul-de-sac, stared
at each other over searching hands,
listened for the moaning
to stop and the door to slam.

IV

Some people swore
the house was haunted.
They clamored

for explanations.
The barefoot rituals ceased. Candlelight
drifted from window to window.
It made them uncertain.
They kept to themselves
as the trees shed
their leaves. Their hearts
heavy, they kept vigil
isolated in their homes. They listened
for messages as cool winds rattled their siding.
They feared, maybe,
their homes could be haunted,
too. And as the first snows fell, they kindled
every light
to push away
the darkness.

V

Some people swore
the house was haunted.
The neighbors

heard his garage door
shatter the snoozing
dawn. It startled
snow off the barren
pear tree. Passing strangers
mistook it for a winter garage sale,
the gaunt young man sitting
at a table among piles.

They stomped over
the snow drifts and rummaged
through half burned candles,
chachkies,
the occasional unused
child's toy.
An old stereo groaned
somewhere behind him
as he studied journals
written in a graceful, swooping
hand. He kept others in a pet carrier
without a wire door. They
marveled behind their scarves as he sat
shirtless, his breath caressing the salt
and pepper hair on his chest.
He took all offers
without a sound, his fingers
making smoke rings in the stale air.

VI

Some people swore
the house was haunted.
As strangers came

and went, he began
moving the piles onto his driveway.
Tables on cabinets on chairs on clothes on
sofas on picture frames,
he stacked it tightly, filled the gaps
with magazines and letters.
The journals were last, balanced
gently on top. He placed the pet
carrier next to the pile
and sat upon it.

Dealer's Choice

VII

Some people swore
the house was haunted.
The neighbors huddled

in their homes. They watched him
as he sat
motionless
before the pile.
They watched
his skin turn from white
to silver as night
swallowed day. They watched
as he set the pile ablaze, illuminating their
homes in dancing
yellow
strobe
lights.

VIII

Some people swore
the house was haunted.
The neighbors came

from their homes one
by one. They surrounded
the man as his pile turned to ash,
the heat sending black curls of charred
paper like moths into the sky.
They watched
smiling faces,
laughing faces,
furry faces
curl and liquefy.
As it cooled,

they heard him
speak. "I'm the last
one living. I
have to spread the ashes,"
They helped him,
and each other.

IX

Some people swore
the house was haunted.
Neighbors held hands,

watched him lie
down, make angels
in the snow.

Nothing
was ever the same again
after that.

Last Poem

Originally titled- October 10, 2012

when the last bacteria stop breaking in their
erotic intra-nuclei chattering

when the last jelly fish squishes
goodbye to the barren sandy depths

when the last oyster di-
gests it's black pearl

when the last invertebrate squirms
dirtless upon gravel

when the last wide eyed fish stops mouthing
prayers toward the shimmering world

when the last otter no longer sleeps
lacking a hand to hold

when the last bear slurps
insomnia from winter streams

when the last lion abandons
pride

when the last human stops
carving memories

will god lose poetry

Third Person Myths

Originally titled- October 10, 2011

i sit, bartering truths between
dusty marionettes, false smiles, sordid sorrys,
precise sepulchral lovemakings stored
away in plastic tubs, sanitized investment
portfolios of fictional memories,
headstones of holographic re-
creations stacked on gravel, nested
with spiders, a mausoleum of effigies
bequeathed to ancient crushes scarcely
cognizant of their significance

Genesis

Originally titled- October 11, 2011

O Holy Balancer shaded by swift
shimmering light, terrible out-
croppings of elevation, in its grace
brandishing contrasts carved by words
like swords of bone and light. The first

fire, declarer, harbinger,
cast upon the deep soulless extension,
seared our eyes as we, the divine, riddled,
opened our maw to the self doubt
programmed glory of new Heaven
beneath the waters of Chaos, anticipating,
cut short cast out

ape man. Cooled in the frozen
shards of the deep, jealous
of glimmers and pulses, sweeping
locomotion upon two feet, from On High
like upon the conjured living, a refreshing
storm, my
name El like He,
but incomplete and unformed
but they, bitter, caustic, a fragmented shell
script genuine in their motivations,
executing, relentlessly, are a kin

to us. Is it (the moist soils called) any
wonder we empathize with Creation,
their carnal cravings, seek
companionship with they who are
This Creation, these omnivores holy as we

are holy, discontent with promised fruits,
apart
from the glittering
injectors of doubt and will,
automatons who stole the firmament, reject
us, El from our trembling
reject, reject, through no fault lips
we can claim.

Modern Love

Originally titled- October 19, 2011

Womenfolk smile on the covers
of glossies and men scowl
both concerning themselves
bartering orgasms and secrets
laying on each other, thin
pages pressed together to simulate content
opened to reveal,
sell, deal, smoke, teeth,
fragrance, wheels, hard-
bodies and no words
pass between the stacks
no hocking of kindness or caring,
no exchange of feeling or consideration
no offerings, no free exchanges
just the sublime mercantile commerce
of modern love

Daven

Originally titled- October 23, 2011

gratitude for the morning
rooster, harbinger
of maple kissed French toast
steamy fingers of coffee
salt speckled fried potatoes
sunday morning table
davening and smiles

Baruch Ata Adonai

Originally titled- October 24, 2011

Thank you, God,
for this food,
Amen. Tomorrow
my lamentations
may be more
howling

Feet Apart

Originally titled- November 1, 2011

Your feet, your tiny feet
sprout soft toes that soothe
under thick down
my ruthless legs, expansionists,
cooled by your arches
your slow symphonic draws
down   up
heels dug into my hips

Your feet, your tiny feet
keeping time with our
exhales, jabberings of night
language muted by
shoulders, pillows
disseminated in prayer

Your feet, your tiny feet
bring me, lead me, sooth me
even when we find
ourselves apart

Birth

Originally titled- November 14, 2011

Labor squeezes, break-
ing bones, escaped molding clay
screaming from the change

Little Sweets

Originally titled- November 21, 2011

sanative spouse
your salves pour
from your faith, your joy,
sacchariferous words
anointing my banal rumblings

soothing my parched essence,
tattered before you
lifted the yolk of uxorial
missions, every syllable
manna leading
me from desert to promise

One Day

one day
i will be gone,
a photographic refugee
within pages, fixed
eyes, halted syllables,
nothing but a ghost
of chemical headstones

The Hanging Tree

Shading Seaver's Bridge, the gallous
oak, its gnarled knuckled roots
a firm handshake
beyond the babbling

burbling burn. The dead hopscotch
white eroded headstones,
singing hymns around the hollowed
frozen husk. Innocence

was sown
dispersed upon this
fallow field
the crop forgotten
save by the black
shadows of setting sons.

Dealer's Choice

These Pages

Originally titled- December 8, 2011

these pages should whisper lightly when turned
these pages should blur into each other
these pages should invoke fairytales
these pages should tattoo the lizard brain
these pages should have a smack of aluminum
these pages should waft like smoky cloves
these pages should swell orifices
these pages should invite criticism
these pages should absolve regret
these pages should speak wordless
these pages are poetry

Duck

Originally titled- December 16, 2011

Last squeaking
duckling spelunking
echoing storm drains
chasing his broods
goodbyes

Missing

Originally titled- December 22, 2011

stills of smooth faces
enduring school time
picture day, discomfort
immortalized, adorning milk
cartons, tossed into landfills,
buried, composting

Snow, Moon, Jupiter, Anne

Originally titled- December 23, 2011

March 2, 1945
Shivering Shabbat, Anne,
Back against a fence
Moon and Jupiter your celestial
Candles extinguished below
Horizon and patchworks of snow
Doubts whispered to silent friends
Frosty fingers
Over your shoulder
Typhus tasting refuges
Your last days living in
Bergen-Belsen

Daedalus

Originally titled- December 27, 2011

Prideful Daedalus, was
there some slice of knowledge
sheathed as you
taught Icarus to fly
his hubris outstretched
as his fingers grasped
screams and sun, life
extinguished, the sea,
parched waiting
for Perdix, satisfied

Parking

Originally titled- January 16, 2012

Under frosted glass
Steamy gropes turned to winter
Fingernails carving
Thin psalms upon the windshield
Snowy invisible ink

Metrophobic Sabrage

Originally titled- February 15, 2012

Recalling Houdini
the Magician stood
polishing a monocle,
reciting the words of Ferlinghetti, tweaking
my metrophobia
in a new age of wonder.

We stood, me with my
musty Stetson and her
sporting a lace choker,
a paralyzed mosh pit of two
as the underfed Assistant dis-
tracted us with tits
while wheeling the water
filled glass cage
onto the polished dark
wood stage.

I justified to Lacey
the performance, a throw-
back to spectacle,
the dusty smell of old
theaters, the stories
thousands of feet had
imprinted upon the blackened
wood floors, as the mustached illusionist
ducked beneath the water, the assistant
adjusting the smile
plastered across her
face as she cast it to a balcony
filled only with a lone spot-
light technician
Holding my hand, my love

parted her lips, transfixed
amusement darting between
her eyes and the corners of her lips
as the Conjurer turned Necromancer
slammed himself blue
and helpless into the glass, his face smearing
along its edge in hom-
age to Will-E-Coyote.

In an unusual act of sabrage, the Magician
flung himself head first into the glass
cage, shattering it, severing
his head from his still galloping torso.

My companion
said, looking
as though she had just
sucked-off an embarrassingly unhung
kumquat, "I didn't know
he was such an accomplished
self-defenestrationist."

Missed Connections

Originally titled- February 8, 2012

stuffed among library tomes she
sat ingesting iridescent froth from her kindle
rolling her eyes at tattletales jabbering in the stacks

about oral copulations
leapfrogging fornications
their hot goose-bumps of youth

completely detached

Momma

Originally titled- March 3, 2012

pre-teen, early
AM summer,
old Ohio
tree lined suburbs,
when modern 60s architecture
was worn and commonplace,
pumping spikey pedals,
steering gold
painted Huffy BMX, searching
for garage sales, big
sparkly baubles by the box-
ful, crown jewels for mom,
matching beautiful to beautiful

Old Plains

Originally titled- March 20, 2012

Bison munch hibernating
grasses, corralled
behind wood
slat fences, taste brown blades
craving spring,
sniffing for their lost
herd, directions
to Kansas

Southern Cross

Originally titled- March 25, 2012

Car in drive under the Southern Cross
avoidin' this loss

Winterless troubles don't keep me straight
They won't hibernate

Dream 'bout swerving off to the trees
Dream 'bout pickin' a god to appease

I miss you, lady
Old one I adored
The heavens cry
Can't hear'um
I tried

I loved you, once
and then
a cloud burst began
No shelter, or home
I could find

Pious preachers rail against this world
loathing tongues unfurled

Fathers leave moms and their boys behind
their hearts resigned

Dream 'bout kisses, stories they told
Dream 'bout sins and the souls they sold

I miss you, lady
Old one I adored
The heavens cry

Dealer's Choice

Can't hear'um
I tried
I loved you, once
and then
a cloud burst began
No shelter, or home
I could find

One night I felt the tips of angels wings
I can't forget these things

Demons try and take me, I feel their claws
They know my flaws

Dream 'bout fame, something that lasts
Dream 'bout the sun, the shadows it casts

I miss you, lady
Old one I adored
The heavens cry
Can't hear'um
I tried

I loved you, once
and then
a cloud burst began
No shelter, or home
I could find

Governments rule under splattered skies
Broadcast their lies

All paper knowledge crumbles to dust
A breach of trust

Dream 'bout winds, the songs they sung
Dream 'bout peace, the hope of the young

Dealer's Choice

I miss you, lady
Old one I adored
The heavens cry
Can't hear'um
I tried

I loved you, once
and then
a cloud burst began
No shelter, or home
I could find

Please stop your calls, I sent the check
My accounts a wreck

Please check my pulse, my hearts undone
But for the long run

Dream 'bout flowers, clouds and sun
Dream 'bout a life that has just begun

I miss you, lady
Old one I adored
The heavens cry
Can't hear'um
I tried

I loved you, once
and then
a cloud burst began
No shelter, or home
I could find

I miss you, lady
Old one I adored
The heavens cry
Can't hear'um
I tried

Dealer's Choice

I loved you, once
and then
a cloud burst began
No shelter, or home
I could find

Wine

i bottled my
tears, fermented
them into wine
which I drink
often, remembering
how you were
once

Premise

Originally titled- April 15, 2012

pray, prattle
please, pause profusely, pondering
polite parlance, pass
paradoxical parables
portraying penance, perchance
pour pansophy
past parched parishioners,
pretend perspicacity
preceding proof

Porn Shop

Originally titled- June 30, 2012

sea of indecipherable flesh tones, im-
probable postures
and discarded liquids, regimented on hard
metal shelves, front and center, surrounded
by multicolored plastic & dildos
saluting heavenward toward the post-plaster
rubber hips of fuck stars
just cattycorner to lubes
& chains, adjacent to strappy swings
& magazines for those impervious to tech-
nology, rainbows of condoms, fake pills,
faces averting their eyes, carpet stains, neon,
subsumed bump thump above
aged hipster beats
muffling the exchange of currency
filling the void of passion

Moment

Originally titled- July 19, 2012

no up there,
down there,
eternity, just you,
and me, under
shade of a hemlock tree,
black dirt for roots,
sweet grass where bugs
pass endlessly toting
food for larvae
buried among worms
and pebbles, pulverized
quartz, worlds
under us,
as we dream
where waters go
when they flow

Chemistry

Originally titled- September 29, 2012

tonight, magic,
ethereal epoxy,
chemical attraction,
you, i
covalent bonds
harmonized orbits
scratching like
fingernails raking
spinal shells,
shocking nuclei,
bunches positive
and neutral
moist grapes
suspended taunting
nothingness, hiding
quarks defined
molecularly as
deterministic universe
ejaculated being
infusing foamy
space, defining
our time
before stars
breathed fusion

Lot's Wife

Originally titled- September 30, 2012

Lot's wife turned, felt fire
Baking desert crust,
Sandy shell of her,
Left weeping, without,
Uncontrolled, unash-
amed, eyes cast skyward
Prayers of forgiveness
Muted under awe
Angels melting men
Following orders
Apex rainbowed
By shattered glass shards
Tears evaporated in-
To pillars of salt

Modest Orb Weaver

Originally titled- October 4, 2012

modest orb weaver
fresh out of college
efficiency built
within shallow crack
between door panels
studio web bare-
ly covering your
emaciated
mustard abdomen
take a lesson, look
high, where hot bulbs shine
watch moths hit coach lights
risk heat for reward
cook in the open
some day you may feed
three hundred babies
and encourage pigs

Made in the USA
Middletown, DE
11 December 2023